APR 17 75

Insomnia
or
The Devil at Large

Insomnia
or
The Devil at Large

Henry Miller

THE PHOTOGRAPHS
Hoki and Henry Miller in piano bar; Hoki Tokuda reaching for flower.
Christian DuBois Larson, Beverly Hills, California
Hoki and Henry Miller in doorway; Hoki and Henry Miller at breakfast.
Yukichi Watabe, Tokyo
Henry Miller at desk.
Bradley Smith

A Gemini Smith book 🏢 published by
DOUBLEDAY AND COMPANY, INC.
GARDEN CITY, NEW YORK 1974
Copyright © 1974 by Henry Miller and Gemini Smith Inc.
ISBN: 0-385-9037-4
Library of Congress Catalog Card Number: 73-15420
Designed by Bradley Smith and Don McQuiston
Printed in U.S.A.

First it was a broken toe, then a broken brow, and finally a broken heart. But, as I said somewhere, the human heart is indestructible. You only imagine it is broken. What really takes a beating is the spirit. But the spirit too is strong and, if one wishes, can be revived.

Anyway, it was always about three in the morning when the broken toe awakened me. "The witching hour" — because it was at that time I wondered most what she might be doing. She belonged to the night and the wee hours of the morning. Not the early bird that catches the worm but the early bird whose song creates havoc and panic. The bird that drops little seeds of sorrow on your pillow

At 3:00 A.M., when you're desperately in love and you're too proud to use the telephone, particularly when you suspect she is not there, you are apt to turn upon yourself and stab yourself, like the scorpion. Or, you write her letters you never mail, or you pace the floor, curse and pray, get drunk, or pretend you will kill yourself.

After a time that routine palls. If you were a creative individual — remember, at this point you are only a bloody shit! — you ask yourself if it might not be possible to make something of your anguish. And that is precisely what happened to me on a certain day around three in the morning. I suddenly decided I would paint my anguish. Only now, as I write this, do I realize what an exhibitionist I must be.

Not everybody, to be sure, recognizes the anguish I depicted in these crazy water colors. Some look up on them as right jolly, don't you know. And they _are_ jolly in a heart-rending way. All those crazy words and phrases — what inspired them if not a twisted sense of humor?

(Maybe it began long ago, with an-other one, the first one, for whom I bought my first bunch of violets, and as I was about to hand her them they slipped from my hand, and, accidentally (?) she stepped on them and crushed them.) Little things like this can be very dis-turbing when you are young.

Now, of course, I am no longer young — which makes everything all the more disturbing. And, needless to add, all the more ridiculous. Except, mark my words, that where love is concerned, nothing, nobody, no situ-ation can ever be utterly ridiculous. The one thing we can never get enough of is love. And the one thing we never give enough of is love.

"Love must not entreat or demand...." (Hermann Hesse) (I will quote the rest of it later. I have it written on my wall, so there is no danger of forgetting.) Yes, this little phrase, which to some may seem banal and trite, I happened upon at a most critical moment.

"Love must not entreat or demand." It's like asking some one to climb a ladder with hands and feet tied. You have to go through agony before you can accept such sublime truth. The cynic will say it's meant for saints or angels, not mortal human beings. But the terrible truth is that it is precisely the impossible that is demanded of us ordinary human beings. It is we for whom temptation leads to salvation. It is we who must go through the fires — not to become saints but to become thoroughly and eternally human. It is

we with our faults and frailties who
inspire the great masterpieces of litera-
ture. We are full of promise, even at our
worst.

(Amen! End the cadenza!)

   And so we have this reputedly famous
old man (75, no less!) pursuing a young
will-o'-the-wisp. The old man very romantic, the young songstress quite down
to earth. She has to be down to earth
because it's her business to make men
fall in love, do foolish things, buy ex-
pensive gowns and jewels. She lost her
heart, not in San Francisco, but in
Shinjuku, Akasaka, Chiyoda-ku and
such places. That is to say, when she
began earning her daily bread.

   The old man (c'est à dire moi,
monsieur Henri) had rehearsed the
whole scene almost forty years ago.
He should have known the score. He
should have been able to play it by ear.
But he happens to belong to that tribe
of human beings who never learn

from experience. And he does not regret his weakness, for the soul does not learn from experience.

Ah, "the soul"!!! How many letters I wrote about the soul! I doubt if there is a word for it in her language. Heart they have, yes, but soul —? (Anyway, so I would like to believe.) And yet, no sooner than I speak thus than I remember that it was her "soul" I fell in love with. Naturally, she did not understand. Only men, it seems, talk about soul. (It's a sure way of losing a woman, to talk about soul.)

And now we should talk a bit about the Devil, blessed be his name! For he had a part in it, as sure as I live. A very important part, I may add. (Forgive me if I sound like Thomas Mann.) The Devil, if I know him right, is he who says — "Don't trust your instincts. Be wary of your intuitions!" He wants to keep us human—

all-too-human. If you're headed for a
fall, he urges you to keep going. He
doesn't push you over the cliff — he
merely leads you to the brink. And
there he has you at his mercy. I know
him well, for I have had traffic with
him often. He delights in watching you
walk the tight rope. He lets you slip,
but he doesn't let you fall.

    It's the Devil in her, of course, that I'm
talking about. And it was that which made
her so intriguing, so help me God. Her
soul was to me angelic; herself, at
least as she revealed it, was devilish.
Of what ingredients was she made, I
often asked myself. And every day, I
gave a different answer. Sometimes I
explained her by race, background, her-
edity, by the war, poverty, lack of vita-
mins, lack of love, anything and everything I could think of. But it never
added up. She was, so to speak, an "insolite". And why did I have to pin her
down, like a butterfly? Wasn't it enough
that she was herself? No! It wasn't.

She had to be something more, or less. She had to be graspable, understandable.

And how foolish this sounds. Everybody "had her number", it seemed, except me. To me she was an enigma. Knowing myself as I do, I tried to believe that it was all part of my usual pattern with women. How I love the unattainable! But it didn't work, this sort of calculation. She was like one of those numbers which are indivisible. She had no square root. And yet, as I say, others could read her. In fact, they tried to explain her to me. No use. There was always a remainder which I could never figure out.

That smile which she gave me occasionally, like a special gift, I gradually observed she could give to most any one — if she were in the mood, or if she wanted something. And I would go again and again just to watch her hand it out! Go where? Why to the piano bar where she sang nightly and dispensed her charms. (Just as I did

with the other who (9.) "taxied" her clients to
Paradise and beyond. Always thinking,
poor fool, it's _me_ she enjoys dancing with :)
    The old man! How vulnerable he is!
How pathetic! How he needs love — and
how easily he accepts the counterfeit of it!
And yet, oddly enough, the end is not
what you think. He won her finally. At
At least, so he thinks. But this is another
story.
    Night after night it was the bar. Some-
times it began with dinner — upstairs.
I would watch her eat with the same
attention as later I listened to her play
and sing. Often I was the first one at
the bar. How lovely, how enchanting to
receive exclusive attention! (It could
have been any one else, he would have
received the same attention. First
come, first served.)
    Those same songs night after night —
how can any one do it and not go
mad? And always with feeling, as

if delivering her very soul. So that's the life of an entertainer! I used to say to myself. Same tunes, same faces, same responses — and same headaches. Given the chance, I would change all that. Surely she must be fed up with it. So I thought.

An entertainer is never fed up with the game. At the worst she gets bored. But never for long. Life without approval, without applause, without acclaim is meaningless to her. There must always be a sea of faces, silly faces, stupid faces, drunken faces — no matter! But faces. There must always be that starry-eyed idiot who appears for the first time and, with tears in his eyes, exclaims — "You're wonderful! You're marvelous! Please sing it again!" And she will sing it again, as if to him only and never again. And if he is a man of means, perhaps a shoe manufacturer, he will ask her to go to the races. And she will accept the invitation, as if he had bestowed a great honor on her.

Sitting there at the bar, playing the part of Mr. Nobody, I had a wonderful insight into the whole show. Forgetting, of course, that I was a part of it, perhaps the saddest part. One by one they would confess to me, tell me how much they loved her, and I, I would listen as if immune, but always sympathetic and full of understanding.

"Love must have the power to find its own way to certainty...." (Hermann Hesse)

First though one has to learn to battle with the powers that rule the base of the spine, viz, Kundalini's brothers and sisters - in - law.

"Good morning, Fröken, is it per- mitted to touch your puff to-day?" (my alter ego, Herr Nagel, speaking.)

All those beautiful tunes rolling around in my noodle as I roll along in the cab. "What would you like me to sing?" Like Madame

Yamaguchi begging permission to re-
move her drunken husband's shoes.
Why not "Irish Eyes are Smiling"?
Or, "By Killarney's Lakes and Dells?"
Anything with a smile in it so that I
can pretend I'm happy. "There are smiles
that make you happy, there are smiles...."
And why not a dash of Bitters? Sometimes I smiled so much it wouldn't
come off when I went to bed. I would
lie there with eyes closed, smiling back.
Now and then I'd get up and do a low
bow — the bow of extreme humility.
(They have a good word for it in Japanese — I forget what it is now.)
Anyway, it's a back-breaker. What's
more, it keeps you in trim for the
next day's insults. Never lose face!
If you meet with prevarication, in-
dignation, procrastination, hallucination,
falsification, vacillation, or even constipation, keep smiling, keep bowing.
    Despite all the chicanery, all the
frivolity, and mendacity, I believed

the past. Now it's buried, let's dance!
Now it's dead, let's make merry! "What
are you doing to-morrow? I'll call you
around four, O.K.?" "O.K." But there
never was a to-morrow. It was always yesterday.

The day before yesterday was another
matter. I mean her life with others, her
love life, so to speak. Somehow all that
seemed locked in the vault of memory.
Only a stick of dynamite could open it.
Besides, was it really important, really
necessary to go into all that? "Love
must have the power, etc. etc. etc."
Maybe I only thought I was in love.
Maybe I was simply hungry, lonely, a
clay pigeon any one could put away
with a toy pistol.

I try to think — when did I first
fall in love with her? Not the first time
we met, that's definite. If I had never
met her again it wouldn't have both-
ered me in the least. I remember
how surprised I was when she called

in her. I believed (13.) even when I knew she was lieing to me. For every wrong, stupid, treacherous thing she did I could make excuses. Wasn't I a bit of a liar myself? Wasn't I too a cheat, a humbug, a traitor? If you love you must believe, and if you believe you understand and forgive. Yeah, I could do all that but — I couldn't forget. Part of me is a sublime idiot and another part is detective, judge and executioner. I can listen like an obedient child and sing Yankee Doodle Dandy backwards at the same time. I could remember weeks later unfinished phrases and sentences, and fill in the missing parts at will — with variations. Only I refrained from doing so. I wanted to see, and I lay in wait to see, what she would remember to remember.

But she wasn't much for recalling or remembering. She always opened up new fields of exploration, like covering the coffin with spades full of dirt to bury

me the next day, or (15.) the day after. I
didn't even recognize her voice. "Hello!
This is your little friend from Tokyo
speaking." That's how it really began.
Over the telephone. Me wondering why I
should be honored with a call. Maybe
she was lonesome. She had only arrived
a few weeks before. Maybe some one had
tipped her off that I was crazy about the
orient, particularly about Oriental women.
More particularly about the Japanese
woman.

"You really dig them, don't you?"
a pal of mine keeps saying.

The ones I dig most are still in
Japan, I guess. Like Lawrence said in
"Twilight in Italy" — "The whistlers
go to America." There are people who
are born out of time and there are
people who are born out of country,
caste and tradition. Not loners exactly but exiles, voluntary exiles. They're
not always romantic either: they
just don't belong. And I mean —

nowhere.

We carried on quite a correspondence. That is, I did. Her contribution was a letter and a half. To be sure, she never read all my letters, for the simple reason that I didn't mail them all. Half of them are in my quaint old New England chest. Some of them are marked and stamped "Special Delivery". (What a touching thing it would be if some one sent her these after I am six feet under!) Then, to paraphrase my beloved idol I could whisper from above: " My dear Koi-bito, how sweet to read these _rabu reta_ (love letters) over God's shoulder." As the French say — "_Parfois il se prod- uit un miracle, mais loin des yeux de Dieu._ God isn't interested in miracles. After all, life itself is just one pro- longed miracle. It's when you're madly in love that you look for miracles.

Dans mon ame je nage toujours.

And while all this was going on I was taking lessons in Japanese! Not from her— she never had time! One of the first mistakes I made, in trying out my Japanese, was to tell her she looked terrible. I had meant to say "You look lovely." (Like dropping the violets, what!) One thing I quickly learned was that money (Kane) is honorable. It's not just "Kane", but O-Kane. (The O stands for honorable.) On the other hand one's wife is usually referred to as "that ugly, silly, miserable creature". Not to be taken literally, of course. An inverted sign of respect, that's all. Many things are upside down or inside out in Japanese, but you get used to it after a while. Whenever in doubt say Yes! and smile. Never show your back teeth — only your front ones, especially the gold-capped ones. If you meet an old friend whose mother or daughter has just passed away you laugh. That means you feel very sorry.

Very soon I learned how to say "the

one I long for." (18.) (<u>Bojo</u> <u>no</u> <u>hito</u>) And
"<u>bakari</u>" — the one and only one. But
none of those catch phrases advanced me
very far.

The truth is nothing got me very
far. I had shown my hand too soon.
Japanese girl not so romantic, it seems.
Mamma-san and Papa-san pick out
nice husband for Cho Cho-san, man with
pedigree, good job, good health and so
forth. Cho cho-san supposed to like very
much, be very grateful. Some times Cho
Cho-san very sad. Some time she make
<u>seppuku</u> — throw self in river or jump
from skyscraper. (never hara-kiri.)

Henry-san feel very sorry for Japanese woman. He feel like marrying <u>all</u>
Japanese women, whether <u>kire</u> or <u>kirai</u>.
All Japanese women like precious
flowers — to Henry-san. Henry-san
foolish man. Too romantic, too trust-
ing, too believing. Henry-san no experience with Japanese woman. Henry-san
read too many books. Now Henry-san

begin to meet many Japanese women. He begin to understand they don't all look alike, talk alike, act alike, think alike. Some very ugly, some very vulgar, some very stupid, some very silly. Still, Henry-san like Japanese woman. Like better, more better maybe, when she also have Jewish blood or Korean blood or Hawaiian blood. Make flower more exotic. Henry-san always like the exotic, the mysterious woman. Henry-san still a Brooklyn boy. Gomen nasai.

They say the Japanese language is rather vague. But the Japanese mind is very bright, very sharp, very quick. You only have to say a thing once and it registers. There are many things you must never say, to be sure. Tender souls? Thin-skinned would be closer. You're never quite sure if you have caused offense or not. "Did I hurt your feelings?" "Yes, you did not hurt my feelings." The eyes, which are often dark and fathomless, tell more than words.

Sometimes the whole face lights up, but not the eyes. A bit eerie, what!

If it were possible to put my finger on the one element in her which got me I would say it was her eyes. Of themselves they were not so very uncommon; it was what she put into them (or left out) which was fascinating and disturbing. Dark though they always were, they could light up at times as if afire, or they could simply smoulder. Or they could dart flames. Or they could die away, perfectly expression-less, into the recesses of her being. Even when gay there was always a latent sad-ness in them. You felt as if you wanted to protect her — but from what? She herself couldn't tell you. Something weigh-ed on her soul, and had been for a long, long time. One sensed this also when she sang. The moment she opened her throat she was another personality. It was not so much that she put her heart in it, as we say — and she could do that — as it was that her soul came through. "Such a sweet, lovely creature," I often heard people say. True, if you looked only at the mask. In the depths of her being she was a volcano. In her depths a demon reigned. He dictated her moods; he regulated her appetites, her desires, her longings and cravings. He must have taken possession of her early in life — "gamahuched" her, so to speak. (Pure conjecture on my part, of course.)

Some songs she sang in both languages. It always sounded better to me in Japanese some how. Coming home a little swacked on occasion I would say to myself — "Get yourself a bulbul and teach it to sing to you in Japanese." Like that I wouldn't be tortured by the look in her eyes. Imagine it singing "Fly me to the moon"! And how nice to be able, after the umpty-umpth time to wring its neck and throw it into the garbage can.

Those same dotty, sentimental tunes night after night — the thought of any one being able to do that not only

amazed but disgusted me. What endur-
ance it must require! But what in-
sensitivity, too. *Mais, comme on dit, les
femmes n'ont ni gout, ni dégout.* Anyway, despite the repetition, despite the
monotony, I always felt like a star-
fish swimming in the frozen dew of the
moon. I carried my own *orgue de
Barbarie* in my vest pocket. Bubu,
or was it "Bobo," always waited patiently.
My greatest rival was Mah-Jong. Who
would believe it? To stay up all night
and play that stupid game she would sac-
rifice anything, except perhaps a mink coat.
Mah-Jong! *Ennui, douleur, tricherie,
connerie, malaise, malheur, sommeil
and caca partout* — such was my in-
terpretation of it. An understatement.
While they rattle the pieces some snooz-
er in a dark corner whistles "My Japanese Sandman" between his broken teeth.
Anything for a game of Mah-Jong. Un-
believable, but true.

 I can remember when the bloody
game became the rage in this country —

circa 1900, it seems^(23.) to me. Yes, even in Brooklyn they were playing it. I was just a kid then and I liked to handle the pieces. I used to think they were pretending to be Chinks, my folks. It seemed like an aristo-cratic game. Poor people didn't have Mah-Jong sets. Poor people didn't speak Chinese or Japanese. Anyway, the rage didn't last very long. It went out with the rubber plant and the antimacassars or whatever they were called. In those days, fortunately, they didn't have sleeping-and-waking pills. One had to go to work in the morning, head-ache or no headache. Alka-Seltzer hadn't been invented yet. Nor did people write checks to pay their losses.

To get back to the piano bar.... There were, of course, the patron saints, or in modern parlance — the Sugar Daddies. And that all too familiar line — "They don't mean anything, they're harmless." As if they enjoyed paying for imaginary fucks. All respectable looking citizens, supposedly castrated. All with telescopic vision and ants in their pants. All fly-ing to the moon in the key of C minor.

If, as Victor Hugo said, "the brothel is the slaughterhouse of love," then the piano bar is the gateway to the hall of masturbation. Those crazy, sentimental love tunes — all written down in her notebook in English, Japanese, Spanish, Italian, French.... "What now, my love?" "You are all I long for, all I worship and adore." "Call me if you're feeling sad and lonely. Maybe it's late, but just call me!" "Love me with all your heart!" "I wish you love." "Love is a many-splendor'd thing." "Love me and the world is mine." "Our love is here to stay." "I can't stop lovin' you." "It must be him — and I love him." "All of me — why not take all of me?" "More than the greatest love the world has known — this is the love I'll give to you alone." "All the things you are." "After you're gone." "I can't give you anything but love." "I'll cling to a dream from afar." "Let's pretend." "Bye bye blackbird!" "Fascination." "Infatuation." Add Constipation, Equivocation, Prevarication, Lamentation, Fornication and the

Holy Brotherhood of Locomotive Engineers. Take away a Schmetterlink and divide by a Maeterlinck. *A la fin ce fût déplorable.* In other words — "Itchy-koo and Kalamazoo." Or, in Japanese — "Aishite 'ru"! (I love you)

All in all, it was the old problem of the happy lunatic begging for love. "I love you!" If I said it in English it meant nothing. (Who would think, for instance, that a beautiful word like Omanko means cunt?) And if I said it in Japanese it was verboten, because premature. To love. "Easier said than done," she once told me over the telephone. Marry first, then talk about love — that was the general idea. Yet every night, at the piano bar, it was nothing but love, love, love. Rivers of love poured from the ivories; nightingales warbled in her throat, all singing of love among the roses. By one A.M. the joint was steaming with love. Even the roaches were friggin' away between the keys. Love. Just love.

A sweet death. And in Japanese it sounds even sweeter: "Gokuraku ojo."

Beneath the mascara was the shadow of her smile. And beneath the smile lurked the melancholy of her race. When she removed her eyelashes there were two black holes into which one could peer and see the river Styx. Nothing ever floated to the surface. All the joys, all the sorrows, all the dreams, all the illusions were anchored deep in the subterranean stream, in the Tohu Bohu of her Japanese soul.

Her black, sluggish silence was far more eloquent to me than any words she might utter. It was frightening too because it spoke of the utter meaninglessness of things. So it is. So it always was. So it always will be. What now, my love? Nothing. Nada. In the beginning as in the end — silence. Music is the bloody hemstitching of the faceless soul. At bottom she hated it. At bottom she was one with the void.

"Love Forever in Bossa Nova"

And so, after months and months of it, what with the itching toe, the unanswered letters, the fruitless telephone calls, the mah jong, the mendacity and duplicity, the frivolity and frigidity, the gorilla of despair which I had become began to wrestle with the devil called Insomnia. Slip-slopping around at three, four and five in the morning, I took to writing on the walls — broken sentences like — "Your silence has meant nothing to me; I'll outsilence you." or, "When the sun sets we count the dead." or, (courtesy of a friend) — "You would not be looking for me if you had not already found me." or the weather report from Tokyo, in Japanese: "<u>Kumore toki-doki ame</u>." Sometimes just "Good-night!" (<u>O yasumi nasai</u>!) I began to sense the germ of a new insanity sprouting in me. Sometimes I went to the bathroom, looked in the mirror and made funny faces, which frightened hell out of me. Sometimes I just sat in the dark and implored the telephone to ring. Or hummed to myself — "Smoke gets in your eyes." or yelled "Merde!"

Maybe this was the best part of it all, so help me God. Who can say? I had been through it before, dozens of times, yet each time it was new, different, more painful, more intolerable. People said I looked wonderful, was getting younger every day, and all that crap. They didn't know that there was a splinter in my soul. They didn't know that I was living in a satin-lined vacuum. They didn't seem to realize what a cretin I had become. But I knew! I used to get down on my knees and look for an ant or a cockroach to talk to. I was getting tired of talking to myself. Now and then I would take the receiver off the hook and pretend to talk to her — from overseas, no less. "Yes, it's me, Henry-san, I'm in Monte Carlo (or Hong Kong or Vera Cruz, what matter.) Yes, I'm here on business. What? No, I'll only be a few days. Do you miss me? What?

Hello, hello ...." No answer. Line dead.

Jolly business, if you have the guts for it. At my age you get to be an expert. Even Byron with his club-foot couldn't have invented more ways to punish himself than the romantic idiot I had become. With one hand holding my guts from spilling out, I could juggle a ping pong ball with the other. (Referring to the testicles, the Japanese are not satisfied to simply call them "balls" — they're "kintama" or golden balls.) Like money (Kane), as I said before. Never dirty money, but honorable money. (O Kane) Well, if nothing else, I was learning a little Japanese. (Private lessons. Not from her.) And the more I learned the less I understood the Japanese — that is to say, their mind, their spirit, their Weltanschauung. Language-wise, nothing to identify with. Now and then I thought I got a clue. For example: Asahi means morning paper. Asa mara morning erection. Akagai can

can mean a fat clam or a fat cunt,
whichever way you like. But _Aishite'ru_
(I love you) — be careful! Better to re-
cite the Lord's Prayer than to say "I love
you" prematurely. Always safe to smile,
however. Especially when hurt, insulted or
humiliated. The stab comes later, when
least expected. It slips between the ribs
just as smoothly as the hand beneath the
fold of the kimono. And when it comes, the
dagger, the correct response is — "Ah so!"
This covers not only a multitude of sins
but a multitude of crimes.

Paradise is separated from Hell only
by an imaginary line, so it is said.
Ecstasy and despair are "Doppelgänger",
that is to say, brothers under the skin.
Love can be a prison without doors or
windows; one is free to come and go,
but to what avail? Darun can bring
freedom or terror. Wisdom is of no help
when one is in a strait-jacket. So it
is. So it was. So it will be.....

When you can't get the lice out of
your brain try waltzing in the dark.
or get a step-ladder and write her

name in Braille on the ceiling. Then, lying in bed with your hands behind your head, imagine you are blind to her faults and thank the Lord Buddha for his grace and charity. Remember all the beautiful things you might have told her and repeat them like a litany. Throw in a joker, like — "Thank you for always calling me darling." It may not be etiquette but even at long distance it gets them by the short hairs. In a bamboo forest you may get lost but you can always see the stars above. Heaven protects the fool but gives him no rest. He thinks tomorrow is another day, but it never is — it's always the same day, the same place, the same time. It's always stormy weather and the visibility nil. Even if there be no peace, no God, no sunshine, he still believes in miracles. What he refuses to recognize is that _he_ is the miracle.

Does love, true love, entail full surrender? That was ever the question. Is it not human to expect some return, however small? Must one be a superman or a god? Are there limits to giving? Can one bleed forever? Some talk of strategy, as if it were a game. Don't show your hand! Play it cool! Back away! Pretend, pretend! Though your heart is breaking never betray your true feelings. Always behave as if nothing matters. That's the kind of advice they give to the love-lorn.

However, as Hesse says — "Love must have the power to find it's own way to certainty. Then it ceases merely to be attracted and begins to attract."

And then ————?

Then God help us, for what we attract may not be at all to our taste. And what we so longed for may prove to be no longer desirable. And whether we attract or are attracted, all that matters is the one and only. The "bakari". More important than enlightenment is the missing half. The Buddhas and the Christs are born complete. They neither seek

love nor give love, (33) because they are love
itself. But we who are born again and
again must discover the meaning of
love, must learn to live love as the
flower lives beauty.

How wonderful, if only you can
believe it, act on it! Only the fool,
the absolute fool, is capable of it. He
alone is free to plumb the depths and
scour the heavens. His innocence pre-
serves him. He asks no protection.

The
Insomnia
Watercolors

a grand whoop-la!

Oh icy white maiden-head of love's logic!

The gorilla of despair beating his breast with immaculate gloved paws.

A giddy gorilla in a satin-like emptiness! NADA

I am the germ of a new insanity

A freak dressed in intelligible language

the gorilla who feels his wings growing!

A splinter buried in the quick of the soul.

Shaking cobwebs out of the sky.

Insomnia #3, Henry Miller 9/6/66

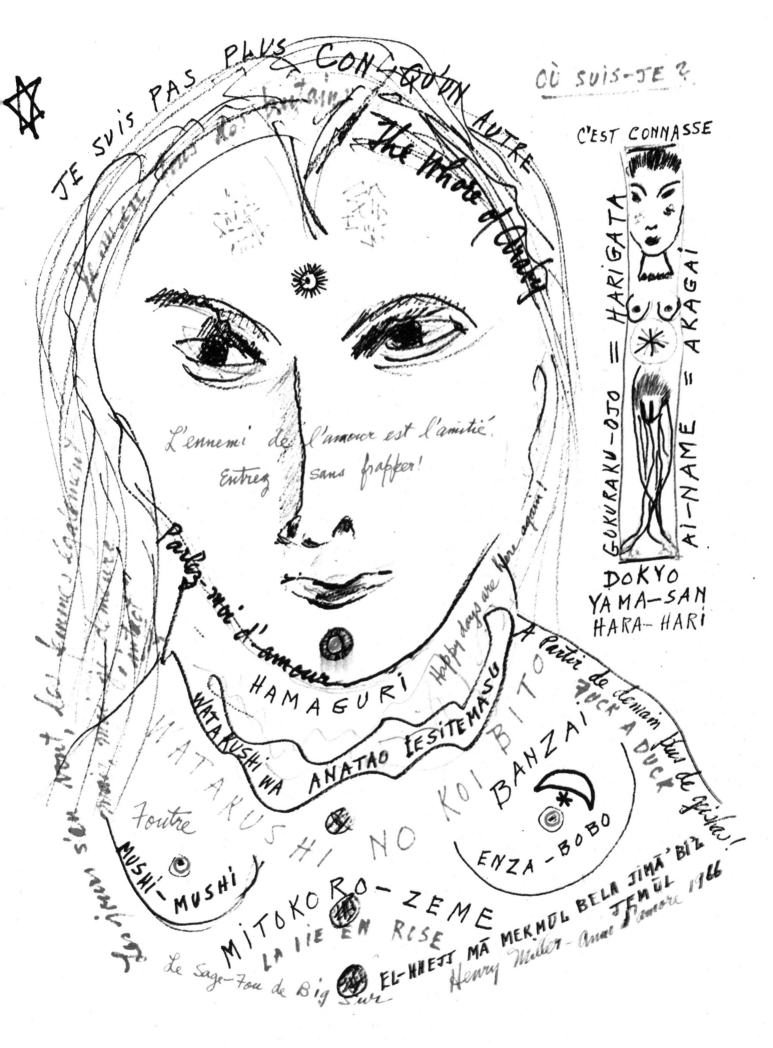

Cadenza

And now a word or two about the reproductions . . .
Fish or fowl? Gruel or Pantagruel? In any case "consubstantial" with the
pervading mania. Or shall we say "adumbrations of nothingness," to
borrow a phrase from a Japanese esthete.

Let us not put Beauty on the chopping block. The illustrative material
which, to repeat, is consubstantial with the nothingness of the subject
matter, makes no claim to beauty, intellect, madness or anything else. It is
of the same fibre as the text, and the key to both is Insomnia. Some of the
illustrations are neither paintings nor drawings, but just words, and often
mere hocus-pocus or gibber-jabber. They reflect the varying moods of
three in the morning. Some were sprinkled with bird seed, some with
songes, and some with *mensonges*. Some dripped from the brush like pink
arsenic; others clogged up on me and came out as welts and bruises. Some
were organic, some inorganic, but they were all intended to lead their
own life in the garden of Abracadabra. None of them are quite *nature
morte*, that is to say—Kosher. All were touched by the Devil's breath and
nothing can purify them but an overdose of lysol.

In principle they illustrate Blake's dictum that "the tigers of wrath are
wiser than the horses of instruction." In their "consubstantiality" they
make a curious amalgam of anguish, cajolery, frustration, melancholia
and absolute nonsense. In other words, so much frivolous horseshit.

On my first trip to Persia, circa 731 B.C., I was impressed by the forlorn
magic created through the marriage of words and figures. A few centuries
later, traveling through the Far East, I was again impressed by the
marriage between love, ethereal love, and illusion. In short, by the
"consubstantiality" of ecstasy and the eternal *tohu bohu* which was later to
be expressed symbolically by the absent pot of gold at the foot of the

rainbow. Aeons later, while in limbo, I discovered the true meaning of the *section d'or* which had so long baffled the ancients that in the Middle Ages the reins were turned over to Hieronymus Bosch, sometimes known as Jerome Bosch.

Much of the technique, the craftsmanship, acquired while sojourning between worlds I was to utilize in the present incarnation. I had learned, so to speak, how to harness ignorance with presumption. I was ready now to become an unacknowledged watercolorist.

My first efforts, begun in the womb, were not too discouraging. There they were, arrayed in all their heraldic pontification, tacked to the cosy lining of the uterus, my mother's own uterus. Nights when I no longer cared to listen to the music of the drains (the maternal pipi, in other words) or pore over the pages of the Talmud provided for prenatal instruction, I would swing blissfully to and fro in the uterine hammock and gaze with foetal glee at my handiwork.

My paintings held a sort of Babylonian fascination for me. As I remarked earlier, they were neither fish nor fowl, neither gruel nor Pantagruel. They just were. And I believe that is how Beelzebub wanted them to be. After all, I was no Cezanne in search of the golden apples of Hesperides.

To tell the truth, I hadn't even decided at that date what sex I was going to be. I was immaculate and hermaphroditic, at least in spirit. Nor had I yet determined whether I would emerge from the cocoon as butterfly or walrus. I was afflicted with musical leanings, I recall. Leanings which were subsequently to lead to my undoing. Yes, little did I realize then what would be the result of my contamination with Humperdinck, Palestrina, Gatti-Cazazza and their spawn of contrapuntalists. Life was still at the cusp, with Venus and Saturn pretending to do the minuet on the starry sward of the zodiac. The cathedrals were still in the offing, the troubadors and matadors, along with Leda and the swan, had not yet been coached to perform their nefarious *amours*. Love was in the air, together with ignorance and folly; the angels danced merrily on superstitious pinheads, but sex was in some other compartment, probably the Black Hole of Calcutta. Hence, *always merry and bright.*

It was about this time that it all began: the flirtation with suicide, the instruction in rhetoric, the near obsession with Joconda, the flight to the Land of Nod, the acceptance of the magic wand, and the choice between Marie Corelli and Petronius Arbiter. Suddenly Turner appears on the horizon, milky as the steed Bucephalus, splashing about in rosy omelettes and architectural washes. The die is cast. Time to emerge from the lair of the womb. Time to wield the brush—first as mountebank, then as *entrepreneur*, and finally as Maestro Rocambolesque who has fallen in love with Rose Tyrien, Chrome Yellow and Mediterranean Blue.

To violate the canons, injunctions and prescriptions laid down by the Royal Academy of Art was fairly easy. Had I not been mothered in chaos, ignorance and bliss? *Kultur* I swallowed in one gulp, always keeping my revolver handy should it dare to raise its nasty head. I became a Dadaist overnight, following the instructions handed down by my unknown master, Kurt Schwitters, the famous Swiss cheese magnate. On the eve of turning Surrealist I suddenly experienced a regression and fell head over heels in love with the old masters. Consorting daily with such as Carpaccio, Fra Angelico, Minnestrone, Uccello and their ilk, to say nothing of della Francesca, Cimabue, Giotto and Masaccio, I unwittingly fell into the trap set by the monks and masturbators of the Dark Ages.

It was during this period that I nonchalantly gave exhibitions, first in June Mansfield's Roman Tavern (Greenwich Village), and later, with the exception of Minsk and Pinsk, in the various capitals of Europe.

In mid-career I revised my technique, a la Rubinstein, in order to curb my predilection for preciosity. Beginning at Bunker Hill, L.A. and continuing on through Beverly Glen, L.A., I made it a point to avoid galleries and museums, pedants and prognosticators. By now my fame had dwindled to such an extent that I was obliged to dispose of my work for trifles such as umbrellas, corduroy trousers, razor blades or anything else I had no use for. The effect was salutary as well as salubrious. I discovered that the important thing was to paint as if I knew nothing, which of course was the case. To paint nothing, or its equivalent, was the next step. Naturally, I never succeeded.

It was during this transitional period that I fell into the clutches of an aberrant astrologer who pretended to read great significance into my work. Born with a caul, he had developed a passion for eschatology before ever finishing primary school. Under the influence of liquor, which was not exactly his cup of tea, he would hold forth until the wee hours on the experiences of the Himalayan masters whose aim it was to bring about the end of history, the resurrection of the flesh and the rebirth of all the avatars from Constantibulus to Spasmodicus Apostrabulus. Under his direction I learned to paint not only with the left hand but blindfolded too. I shudder now to think of the results achieved under the direction of this eschatological fiend. One thing he did accomplish, however, and that was to set me free of the trammels of perfectionism. From this point onward my path led inevitably to the nightingale's nest.

My *uguisu*, as the Japanese call the nightingale, not only possessed perfect pitch but she had also cultivated a taste for the *ukiyoe, shabu-shabu* and the more recondite reaches of the Anglo-Saxon tongue. I was hard put to it to invent something which she had not already seen, read or heard. Of a night when she had drained her repertoire I would go to bed humming one of those sentimental ditties she had inoculated me with. ("More than the greatest love the world has known, this is the love I'll give to you.") Then, shortly before dawn, I would arise from my bed of ecstasy and paint a watercolor to bring her the following evening. I had not reached the Insomnia stage yet. It was all euphoria, punctuated now and then by a wet dream in which the archetypal mother image blended monstrously with the nightingale.

To make things more delirious I had become a Scriabin addict, stirred to the depths by his unresolved fourths and his glittering rainbow-cocaine effects in the upper partials. At the same time I took to rereading Knut Hamsun's romances for the lovelorn, *Mysteries* in particular. Again I fancied myself another Herr Nagel with a violin case full of dirty laundry. On my daily walks around the block I took to repeating that memorable line of his: "Good morning, Froken, is it permitted to touch your puff today?" Anything and everything could set me off, even a Japanese calendar. I was bewitched and bedazzled. I went so far as to buy a majolica piss pot which I never used. I made faces in the mirror when shaving, just to prove to myself that I could look happy and demented if I wanted to.

Finally came the broken toe, the imaginary telephone calls—and Insomnia. I was now ripe for the Swedenborgian phase, the transition, in other words, to the mystico-doloroso *Gestalt*. Angels swarmed about me like drunken pigeons. Languages I had forgotten came to my tongue unbidden and in syntactical perfection. I communed with the departed as easily as with my next door neighbors. Before and after breakfast I went to the synagogue to commune with the late Baal Shem Tov. For lunch it was *Gaspard de la Nuit* in the guise of Gilles de Rais. I had one foot on Jacob's ladder and the other in a cesspool. In short, I was ready to come apart at the seams.

It was in this cacodemonic state that I began the word-paintings which, as I may have said before, are neither gruel nor Pantagruel but "consubstantial," "pervious and maculate." It was in this mood that Maeterlinck and Schmetterlink united in connubial bliss, assisted by houris, divas and odalisques. It was the witching hour when Draco crosses the Ecliptic and transvestites begin to counterfeit carnal love. My lust for the *insolite* and the incongruous was at zenith. I had only to think of a horse, any old horse, and there he was prancing on hind legs with nostrils snorting flames. (And my *uguisu*? Probably polishing her toenails or busy converting her tips into imaginary yen.) Whatever the image which came to mind it was sufficient to exacerbate me and sharpen my vocabulary. As I painted I spoke with her in Japanese, Urdu, Chocktaw or Swahili. I glorified and defamed her at the same time. Occasionally, taking a cue from Bosch, the initiate, I depicted her inside an hour glass crowded with spiders, moths, ants and cockroaches. No matter what the setting, she always looked angelic, virginal and inscrutable.

At five A.M. the alarm usually went off, the signal to take a sleeping pill and call it a day. Usually I slept lightly, still carrying on with the writing and painting, or else inventing crossword puzzles which made no sense. Sometimes I tried to work out my astrological chart for the ensuing months, but without success. Eventually the anima, *her anima*, which had been stalking me, died of inanition. Instead of the nightly scribble-scrabble I took to playing the piano, beginning with Czerny and on through Leschititzky and his stable mate Lord Busoni. I transposed everything to the key of F-sharp minor, and in the process broke all my fingernails. In this manner I finally exorcised the Dybbuk and put him in chancery. I learned to live with my Insomnia and even to enjoy it. The last touch was to liberate the nightingale from her gilded cage and quietly wring her neck. From then on we lived happily ever afterwards, which is the way of true love.

Henry Miller